Recognizing the Other Side

Delano Walker

McClure Publishing, Inc.

Copyright © 2022

Delano Walker for McClure Publishing, Inc.

All rights reserved. Printed and bound in the United States of America. According to the 1976 United States Copyright Act, no part of this book may be reproduced or utilized in any form or by any means, electronic or mechanical, including photocopying, recording, or by any information storage or retrieval system, except by a reviewer who may quote brief passages in a review to be printed in a magazine or newspaper, without permission in writing from the Publisher. Inquiries should be addressed to McClure Publishing, Inc. Permissions Department, 398 West Army Trail Road, Bloomingdale, IL 60108. First Printing: April 30, 2022.

The author and publisher have made every effort to ensure the accuracy and completeness of information contained
in this book.

ISBN-13: 978-1-7347595-8-7
LCCN: 2021921091

Cover Design and Editor Kathy McClure

To order additional copies, please contact:
McClure Publishing, Inc.
www.mcclurepublishing.com
800.659.4908

Table of Contents

Page

Note from the Author
Recognize the Other Side
A Moment of Pride 11
Perfectly Imperfect 13
A Wondering Mind.................................. 15
A Paradigm Shift 16
The Silly Truth....................................... 17
Parachuting my Dreams 19
One of A kind 20
I Am... 21
Martyr... 23
I Got There.. 25
Recognize the Other Side 27
Ain't I a Woman? 31
Hindsight 33
Black Gold.. 34
Black Sunlight 35
She's Becoming 36
Eternal Light 37

Table of Contents

	Page
BLACK PARADISE (PART I)	38
BLACK PARADISE (PART II)	39
QUEEN	41
LOVE IS A VACANCY	42
PRIVATE INVESTMENT	43
I AM BECAUSE WE ARE	44
MAGIC	45
MS. RECOGNIZABLE	47
INTERNAL SCARS	49
NATURAL STATE OF PERFECTION	51
RECOGNIZE THE OTHER SIDE	53
THIS IS WAR	57
AMERICA	59
WHAT ARE WE	61
AGAINST ALL ODDS	62
MISREPRESENTATION	65
CULTURE	69
JUSTICE	71
I KNOW WHY THE CAGED LION ROARS (PART I)	72
I KNOW WHY A CAGED LION ROARS (PART II)	73

Table of Contents

	Page
DESTINY CHANGERS	74
A STATE OF MIND	75
MONUMENTAL	77
BIOGRAPHY	

NOTE FROM THE AUTHOR

Recognizing the Other Side is a poetry memoir. Every poem locates a place in my life that I engaged in mentally, emotionally, and spiritually. On this journey of discernment, there's always an alternative that could be considered. I began to discover what's important is invisible to the naked eye, starting with my spirituality. I didn't say this with spookism in mind. I'm coming from a place of cognizance. My spirit is only energy that vibrates on high and low frequencies and to make sure it functions to the best of its ability, I had to develop it through discipline. Starting with traditional practices that satisfied my flesh rather than liberating my soul, left me empty.

Energy is in everything. It can be good or bad energy transmitting through us and ultimately being passed along to other people. Having all this in mind, I knew that the environment I grew up in, the words I used, what I celebrated, and the people I surrounded myself with either took away or contributed to a bias yet innocent, one way of doing things.

Recognizing the Other Side is about understanding it's always an alternate decision to make and with an open mind, we can discover it. Just because our loved ones and those who were put into position to educate us about our values, principles, and the world we live in doesn't mean what they proclaim to be true is a hundred percent right. When we cross that threshold of adulthood, we are responsible for our actions and when consequences are unavoidable, we won't be excused because our parents, friends, and teachers told us how to resolve future problems. Our lack of not knowing will only be on us and for us to deal with.

Finally, to recognize the other side is realizing that defining who we are can be limited in thought but to imagine what we can become is unlimited possibilities. Let's not be vulnerable without any form of resistance to worldly influences, because it will only lead us to having an identity crisis. Let's make being ourselves the new cool and do so unapologetically, because where the real happiness resides, is being at peace with who we truly are.

RECOGNIZE THE OTHER SIDE

Where those who were dead never died,

but went back to where they derived

and became one with the universe….

Recognize the other side where suns (men)

called their women earth because they'll give birth

to all living things.

Recognize the other side when your conscious awakens,
and you begin to see through your third eye.

Where pride and ego take away from a part of your
all-knowing (spiritual being)

Then bound you in consequences that resulted in
wrongdoing.

Recognize the other side acknowledge it and pay attention
to it.

It has been proven as a fact we are kings and queens.

Our ignorance gave fiction to it.

Born without fathers.
This is common and nothing new.
Raised by women
Who were born from
mothers that didn't
raise them.

A Moment of Pride

It's not mine.
Are the first words that's comes to mind
when told for the first time, he could potentially
become a father.
Why bother taking
a DNA test when her only option is to seek for an
abortion?
This deadly poison eats away at her skin because the
boy
she knew, who pretended to be a man, don't want to
be a father.
Now she's stuck to illustrate a single parent while the
co-author
of this story
has become a shiny example of what's being televised
daily
on, Maury.

Perfectly Imperfect

I am not perfect.
Never will be.
I treated family like friends, friends like family.
I craved for fame because I had a taste of popularity.
I lived in falsehood because I was afraid of parenthood.
I once was the main reason women said, "Men are no good."
I am a class X felon who is now outcasted from mainstream society.
Youth will no longer hide me from responsibilities and being alive has
assured me, this world will eventually kill me.
I often wonder if I'm a lifeguard to a race that is drowning from a sea of discrimination. I can't help but to think
I'm just as bad as law enforcement.
Who will protect me
if I felt my life was in danger?
I told you I wasn't perfect.
Appreciate my value as a human being because I am not worthless.
My community, my upbringing, my mistakes, my decisions, and
my logic has derived from a ghetto comprehension.
My whole life I've been placed in a box that's under suspension,
like I'm incapable of doing right without gaining negative attention.
Like I'm incapable of being faithful to a woman without
practicing a religion.

Like it's impossible to be a father to multiple children.
Why base your assumption off of
what you can see and rule over the possibility of
what's invisible?
I bleed like you bleed.
I feel pain like you feel pain.
Yet, because of the way I look, I am treated like we
are not the same. That's a damn shame.
I am not perfect and never
will be.

A WONDERING MIND

So much pain in my bright smile.
I was focusing on the future of you, my young child.
Strongly doubted that you weren't mine because your
mother was a problem that I left behind.

Hope you forgave me for the times we didn't share,
for the life that I chose that wasn't fair.

Your mother said you know me because she showed
you pictures, but it's nothing like seeing your face and
spending time with you.

I guess she was afraid of giving you my last name.
Too ashamed of my illegitimate
claim.

The wiser I got, I felt
unhappy because I missed a precious opportunity to
be a good father.

My heart goes out to all the real fathers who were
there to hold
their sons and daughters' bottles.

Continue to keep pushing and make it work,
because if being there can make your children lives a
bit better,
not being there can make it a lot worse....

A Paradigm Shift

Light eclipsed my vision
the day I acknowledge your existence.
I had never seen serenity so vivid.
And with the coming of you, my life shifted.
A child of my own, such a blessing I was gifted.
My chance to love someone so innocent,
challenged my heart of stone.
The day you accompanied me, I knew I'd never be alone.
Before then,
I'm on my own without a purpose.
I know I'll never be perfect, but I'll strive towards it because you're worth it.
All I know for certain is that I am all yours
To keep and rely upon in any situation.
Guidance in unfamiliar territories despite my detours.
In these foreign places (jail).
I'll never let that path be yours to trace.
Nor will I ever let our time be others to waste.
While love develops in my heart and waits patiently to be expressed,
I'll continue to work on becoming
a better father and a better man.
You deserve the best.

THE SILLY TRUTH

I once was hidden by deception.
I thought the truth would never find me.
Pride, hate, and anger clutched on my soul,
and then dictated my pace because I lack self-control.
My presence was someone else's.
My spirit no longer wanted to live inside my skin
because my fleshly desires
revealed how soon my existence will come to an end.
I'm surprised I'm still breathing.... My rights and
wrongs are selfishly defined.
If given an opportunity to stand in front of honesty,
I would've preferred to stand behind.
What I thought was the truth,
proved to be only in my mind.
I was an object of deceptions, an instrument of lies.
What if I told you
I epitomize these traits to survive.
Your reply; "That's a sob excuse!"
I have to disagree.
Better yet,
when I turn my back, you'll say, "Silly me."
Silly me for going through
trials and errors to understand neighborhood barriers,
are what shaped my mentality.
Silly me for being under resourced and not having a
male voice inside of my
household.
Silly me for seeing my brother (Marcus)
laid out in cold blood and knowing
who it was, dishonored their service and protection.
Silly me if I told you America is not the exception,
because some days I'm treated as if I'm under third

world oppression.
Silly me if I told you these truths.
Judging me are seeds of personal opinions that will never bear the truth.
Silly me....

Parachuting my Dreams

Sometimes, I ask myself,
is it too late for me to spread my wings
since I've been caged by my own limitation?
Is it too late for me?
Since I am locked behind a door that helped enforce
rules and regulations.
Is it too late for my patience?
I trust myself to guide me in a world, influenced by
one click of a button.
Will it be best for me to stay afraid of absolutely
nothing?
Should I awake from sleeping because I am alive?
When time calls for me
to ready my wings,
will I fall flat on my face
since I've never been able to thrive?
Is it too late for me?
I scream!!!
Is it too late for me?
I cry,
"Is it too late for me?"
I dream,
"Is it too late for me?"
If not today, then one day
I will ready my wings.

ONE OF A KIND

Your love and care
has polluted the air.
I'm happy to be moved by your passion.

Your conscious for the unconscious, has kept me aware
when violence and destruction became my distraction.

Your vision for the blind has opened my eyes
to recognize what's already happening.

Your mind was greater than what anyone has imagined.

You are the gift to the Spirit that's
forever lasting....

                Attribute to Maya Angelou!!!

I AM

I am a picture worth a thousand words, framed by society and placed
on a shelf, where nothing else stands beside me.
I am a product of my environment. Unemployed is not employed.
Which means death is an early retirement.
I am time moving at its regular pace.
I will not stop, and I will not wait.
I am a gift to the present and a surprise to my future.
I am the praise in the church when the choir sings, hallelujah!
I am one of many goals my people struggle to achieve.
I come from the truth (Yahweh/God) that nobody has to believe.
I am a part of a dream.
Not any dream, one that Martin Luther King Jr. envisioned 61 years ago.
I am hope and faith threaded into every fiber of his being.
I am sacrifices and contributions made for my existence.
I am the words echoed from Malcom X,
By any means necessary, I will stand
up for what I should be resisting (inequality). I am a creator of my legacy and destiny.
Therefore, I am a manifestation of my ancestors' integrity.
I am an extension of myself.
If it wasn't for them, it wouldn't be no me.
I am eternal....

Martyr

Take my life, before
you take away the innocent.
I'm guilty for doing wrong.
Desert me before you abandon our children.
I accept where I belong.
They deserve a fair chance.
A boy matures into a man.
A girl blossoms into a woman.
This cycle is everlasting.
A mother to be,
carries a baby in her womb and the father of that
child has an opportunity to express love with a
passion.
And I am asking:
Don't shoot.
Give our kids a fair chance.
Why multiply the odds
against us for foolish pride? We're impulsive to
defend.
From afar, I witness your trembling hands.
I wish I could've asked you,
"Why kill someone you don't understand?"
Why are we so blind to seek revenge?
As if that child that stands
next to your enemy doesn't exist.
As if spitefulness is total
bliss and the risks are greater than the reward.
It's necessary
for me to remind you their eyes crave to see more.
Their wings haven't soared, and their hands want
more than what their arms can reach for.

Yet, you think for
Yourself.
Your pleasures.
Your desires.
Your instant gratifications you've become accustomed
to.
Coming to terms with the mentality,
It's better for them
than me
can make a family traumatized.

You allowed the world
to see that you don't think above your waistline.
And what's on your waistline, determines our
children's fate.
You're worse than a judge viewing a case and still
sentencing an innocent black man to life without
parole.
Therefore, I must say you should feel successfully
ignorant
because you accomplished your goal.
So, the next time you decide to shoot, find somebody
like
me to publicize your truth.
The next time you decide to shoot, find somebody
like me to publicize your truth.
Now, what are you waiting
for?
Shoot.

I Got There

I finally arrived at a place only courage lived.
My mind begged me to bring fear along, but I refused.

I refused to give control to an emotion that will determine my direction.

I've learned to hold my head high during failure while never doubting that I would succeed.

Time has become sand I tried to grip
but has fallen quickly through my fingers.

Leaving me to absorb my consequences.

If I was hugged with a gentle squeeze,
guilt would've poured out and strengthened my knees.

Fortunately, this place of courage has given me a chance to be brave.

Although criticism won't cease, fear will never invade.

Now my spirit is unafraid
of words and undefeated by flesh.
Instead, high, and free
like a bird living outside of its nest.

This place where I arrived, I encourage humanity to pursue because it makes a difference believing in yourself while fulfilling what Yah created you to do.

RECOGNIZE THE OTHER SIDE

Not by force, but by the choices we were all given.
Acknowledge the strength it takes to endure
experiences
constantly seen.
Step away from preconceived notions and biases that
doesn't give
them a fair chance.
Understand what it takes to be a woman and what it
takes to be men.
Don't glance. Don't peek.
Look as long as it takes to register a woman.
Worth is priceless and our actions against them
shouldn't be
so cheap.
It's impossible to compile who they are
in these selections of poems.
But I encourage you
to read on, on and on.

Where is they shield?
Where is they knight in shining armor?
Every woman is a Michelle to a man who had
leadership like President Obama.

AIN'T I A WOMAN?

In my life, I witness women fulfilling
a speech Sojourner

Truth spoke.

With every muscle inside their bodies, they epitomize
the profound quote, "Ain't I a woman?"

As if nothing is off limits and honestly speaking, it
shouldn't.

Women who are underpaid and can do the very thing
her male co-worker can do.

What's rightfully given to him should be rightfully
given to her.

Why become a stay-at-home Mom,
collecting crumbs from the government's slices of
American Pie?

Nowadays, men are more insecure than ever before.
They said, women can't — then women did.
Perhaps it's a woman's credit score, their ability
to express themselves without displaying much
emotion that keep us men on the edge of our seats
wondering:

Will she extend her reach
and climb over stereotypes that reveal her
capabilities?

Delano Walker

Will this make her self-reliant?
Since she knows her worth, Will she remain in compliance?

This country is male driven, but some way, somehow she found a way to make a living.

Ain't she a woman?

Didn't Yah create her to walk around for nine months with a baby in her stomach?

It's our job as men to protect
her with the power we hold within.

At first, I didn't understand,
now I do.
I can't imagine a blue sky without you.

I can't imagine not having a sound judgment during a financial crisis.

I can't imagine not having balanced emotions showcasing devotion,
wrapped into a sincere effort.
I can't imagine....

I can't imagine if you ever get under a lot of pressure,
stay calm because thus far
you have displayed what most women truly are ...

Matriarchs.

HINDSIGHT

My beautiful sisters
you don't have to stand alone my enemy is myself
I have no discipline
I tear you down to feel good on the inside
but that's not who I am that's only my pride
I search for love and stumble across your heart
I am not responsible. I abuse your affection
and believe sex was the answer to all your questions
while laying between your legs and planting seeds in
your stomach.
then I'll run when you say a child is coming
look it's me who should stand alone
I disrespect you with unkind words
money is my passion
I fall in love with everybody else's, including mine
and treat something that's priceless like nickels and
dimes
Don't stay because I have
money to give, money shouldn't be your master
Become true to who you are and believe it's true
A goddess to this world most boys never knew
A queen to an empire most prince gives up.
A woman to a society that's bigger than a quick fuck.
Regardless of my lack of leadership, be what you are
destined to be
because boys will keep you caged in
but men will set you free.

BLACK GOLD

What's a fire to a woman who sees her way through it, unscathed?
Unwavering faith,
might bend but won't break.
She's brave.
Her voice is behind issues most women won't talk about.
Hashtag her too!
This society won't see her coming.
A black wonder woman, little girls are inspired.
They believe the closest thing to purification
is getting through a fire.
She carries the torch
that many women held before her and will pass it along to those
who will come after.
She's what most of us chase after and can eventually catch up with.
A sister, who isn't afraid to commit
but will like reciprocation of that same dedication.
A sister who's self-inspired
but can use a brother's motivation.
A sister who struggles
to keep her integrity intact and embraces her natural beauty.
She is proud of her Blackness. A sister....

BLACK SUNLIGHT

There is a glow about you that connects with my heart as if you were standing still and I was drawing you before realizing the similarities the poser has with its artist all lie in a beauty of art.

You stole the spotlight from the sun when you rise
It feels like I am extracting energy from a star.

Empowered by the energy of your galaxy,
my soul arrived at a place where only love dwells
pleading and hoping my heart hatch from this physical shell.

I disregarded my flesh
so my spirit can excel.
Now I am your moon reflecting your light
and you are my day, and I am your night.

Black sunlight.

SHE'S BECOMING

The first lady of a woman:
She's buzzing like bees on honey.
She's nothing, men, like we have imagined...
Too beautiful for beauty pageants
and she slays like a trained assassin.
She's struggling gracefully.
She moves at the speed of womanhood
and boy, oh, boy,
as a man child, I wouldn't ask her to wait for me.
She's beautiful, smart,
and publicly educated.
Down to earth, and grounded by her ancestry.
She witnesses the legacies of Michelle Obama,
Alicia Garza and Tarana Burke.
She's first, and after her there's no more.
Cherish her presence. Men have minded her essence,
placed prices on her possession and came up empty
handed.
She's assertive, invaluable, and driven by purpose.
She became her habits of her day-to-day life.
She licenses to be unapologetically herself and
reserves the right.
And that right she preserves.
She is our words, now choose them carefully.
She's becoming....

Hope, happiness, and love.
She is forever present,
what's to come and once was.
She is eternal....

ETERNAL LIGHT

Eternal light, darkness has come to you
in many different shapes, forms, and sizes.
So, I hope it dawns on you like when the sun rises:
We count on you to shine through.
My wish is for only peace to find you.
My hope is for love to not
blind you from a man that's worthless of it.
Dare him to love you out loud.
If it's expressed in secret
Queen, you don't need it.
And he can keep it.
Eternal light, there's meaning to your existence.
Conviction in your sentences.
Such as, I am beautiful, I am phenomenal
and powerful.
I embody the purpose God created me to
be, which makes me accountable.
I am the light!
Sometimes I shine bright.
Sometimes I am dim and sometimes
I flicker.
Yet, this is who I am.
The sunshine in your blue sky.
The bright idea that comes to mind when in search
for creativity.
I am never too far and never to near.
I am perfectly there, and once my flesh disappears,
my spirit will be
eternally here. You are the eternal light.

BLACK PARADISE (PART I)

Black paradise
when I'm in your presence.
I can vividly imagine the garden of Eden.
Give me a reason, at least one, why your heart
isn't a tree I shouldn't eat from.
You are fresh fruit from a living soul.
Black paradise, your heart is fertile.
Fertile enough to cultivate a vision.
We'll blossom into what's
meant to be.
So, allow nature to take it's
course, while this unseen force shows our spiritual
makeup.
Black paradise,
there's an afterlife for our existence.
Every seed I plant in your
heart symbolizes my commitment.
Which will last in another lifetime.

Black paradise,
being yourself is enough for me to cherish.
Finding peace with or without me
is important enough for me to encourage.
I had to let you know or else I wouldn't be the same.
If I robbed you about how you make
me feel,
it wouldn't be a fair exchange.
Black paradise when I'm in your presence.

I can vividly imagine

the garden of Eden.

BLACK PARADISE (PART II)

Black Paradise,

everything in this world that we love, we may have to sacrifice.

Depending on how we live now determines our afterlife.

Come build heaven on earth with me.

If you don't believe I exist in your world, come search for me.

Black Paradise, I am in everything yet, perfectly imperfect.

Too deep to be seen on the surface.

Too spiritual

to be born without a purpose.

Forever will I be at your service. I am the truth.

Don't listen to a serpent.

Black Paradise, Let's be fruitful, multiply and replenish the earth.

You are a blessing. Who told you that you were a curse?

Dr. King wouldn't be as successful

if it wasn't for Coretta.

Malcom wouldn't have been any better if it wasn't

for Betty Shabazz.

Barack wouldn't have been the president if it wasn't for the woman he has.

Shout out to Michelle Obama.

I wouldn't be the man that I am if it wasn't for my mother.

Black paradise,
I want to be your significant other.
The man that waits for you at the end of the isle
watching your tears of joy
turn into a beautiful smile.

Black paradise, I want you to be the woman that carries my child.

QUEEN

You my queen
through your actions I believe
you'll show me what true love means
and if maybe I can grab hold to it and just squeeze
I won't wait until
I fuck up to get on my knees
Your affection will motivate me to do so
You know words such as from the very first day....
Eye to eye contact before reaching for your finger
while your body awakens from a reality that once
made you a dreamer
Will you....
These moments await us like
off days at work,
like desperate fans who watch to see what team
comes in first.
These moments are created every time we are
together and hope these days last forever and ever
and ever.

You my Queen....

LOVE IS A VACANCY

Love is a vacancy
until somebody moves in,
and you hope it will work
for the second time.

What's about to start in seconds,
could possibly end.
So, you want to be certain
before you take it all in.

Jealousy can't hide,
hate can't stand it
and envy is screaming out loud
for you to end it.
But don't
Love searches for the highest understanding.
The enemy is always trying to take advantage,
pull us from our roots that God has planted.
So, even when you're humble
and living by righteous standards,
opposition will try to treat you like
a door and knock you off the hinges....

What happens when
love is stranger and it's hard to be its friend?
It knocks on the door, but you won't let it in.
You're sick and tired of being abandoned, but you
send signals that you're comfortable being alone.
For this reason,
love is a guest and it'll never feel at home.

I guess love is a vacancy....

PRIVATE INVESTMENT

How can I withdraw
from a person I wholeheartedly invested in?
From this day forward,
I needed you to be not only my woman,
but my accountant.
Keep records on a day-to-day basis of my love.
All I ask for in interest is yours in return.
Trust for our love to grow and we'll become wealthy
in spirit.
Until death tears us apart,
this world will never experience bankruptcy.
Nor will it ever experience another great depression.
I promise!
I promise I won't be your mistake, so people can say,
"I hope you learned your lesson." You are my public
investment.
I want to become a shareholder for every emotional stock
you possess.

I hope I am not considered greedy for voicing my opinion
on soulful capitalism.

Because love is a business of its own,
and I'm happy you allowed me to become an employee
that had the chance to earn
every emotion inside your heart.

I AM BECAUSE WE ARE

What are we to be?
Unforgettable and significant.
For every moment we share together, we dare the
history books to mention it.
From the very essence of our innocence, love will be
expressed in its purest
form.
Now that we know why we are
together,
it became as important as the day we were born.

What are we to be?
As beautifully spoken as this poem:
Elegant.
Unduplicated.

Our lives will be forever indebted to each other.
Becoming one in spirit is our only compensation.
Despite opposite sexes, we'll form a union of duality
by exceeding our physical to revitalize our spirituality.

This is what we are to be:
One with the galaxies....

MAGIC

This is magic
without the pull back of a curtain.
Only an unbelievable occurrence.
Who saw us then, now see love and the magic that's here.
We'll be judged and pointed at in disbelief.
provoking and, oh my God
moment.
Who's to say those who never had it
may even want it?
Sacrifices, responsibilities and broken
relationships from infidelity.
For those who have had it, may always need it.
But who's to say they want to keep it?
Yet, this is magic
and only a few have figured it out.
Love takes its time and won't move too fast.
If it's not happening naturally, unfortunately, it won't
last.
When it happens, it'll be magic and feel supernatural.
Imprisoning your soul with sacrifices
of how that person shackled you.
This is magic.
When questioning
our eyesight isn't necessary and finding your soulmate
can be legendary.

Without the pull backs of curtains, only an unbelievable occurrence.

This is magic.

Ms. Recognizable

Beauty pageants pale in comparison to the very essence of who you are.

Every walk to your destination is similar to slaying red carpets.

For awards giving to movie stars.

Those in awe confuse it with envy
Because of your natural ability to even out the odds.

Like denying a woman who can't raise a boy into a man.

Sure, she will. I know she can.

Only death can sabotage her efforts.

Those who are oblivious claim they never met her
but she exists.

From her grandmother to your mother.
From your sister to your niece.

Imagine a body without water.
Imagine us without women.

The extra motivation that keeps us winning.

The dizzy attractions that keep us spinning
before we fall in love.

Defying physics to keep you ascending
has extended my reach to bring you the stars above.

Ms. Recognizable centuries has passed, and it didn't make you any less valuable.

And no matter what day and age it is,
it never will.

I am humble to say my immaturities has come to an end.

I miss you once, but I will never overlook you again.

Ms. Recognizable....

INTERNAL SCARS

Survivor
Not one of war but sexual abuse.
A child innocence can be toyed with,
and muted into silence.
Leaving children with questions.
They struggle to accept even in private.
Trauma has ruined their special moments.
And disgrace them from smiling.
Eventually suicide is unavoidable,
and the price of living is unaffordable.
Consumed with the idea that their story is not worth
listening to.
Judged by the abuser – the memories of him,
now and potentially forever will sentence more than a few.
To a lifetime of pain.
Moments with significant others feels like intimacy of
shame.
What is it that you gain?
From venom that comes from people not only snakes.
Piecing yourself back together after you were broken.
What difference does it make?
You were a predator of prey, by circumstances and now
have risen above it.
Your survival was necessary to give others a new pair of
eyes to see through.
Your voice was yours but now it is shared by people,
who uses the power of the #MeToo!!!!!
You weren't alone and if it's worth anything, I must say,
we need you!

NATURAL STATE OF PERFECTION

Beauty has no color or shape

Beauty has no color or shape

They're born this way and I embrace their flaws

Her waist isn't small

Her hips are wide

She's perfect this size

You fill in the blank

What is she to you?

Without factoring in the standards

This society has cherished

What is she to you?

When you are trying to define her

Try to do so outside of what's being said on the news

What words would you choose?

Remember …

Beauty has no color or shape

They are born this way

And their natural state of perfection

Makeup is inapplicable

Lipstick is invisible

Her eyelashes are hers

Her curves make a dress more responsible

Than the streets that connect to a curb.

What is she to you?

Unapologetically herself

Seeing her reflection in a mirror is enough to be seen by nobody else

She composes with traits of love and happiness

This and nothing else make her beauty immaculate

What words have you chosen?

To destroy a woman's happiness….

RECOGNIZE THE OTHER SIDE

Recognize the other side
Where service and protection are defined by excessive use of weapons.
Where laws don't apply to a certain group of people
And what is considered to be illegal is legal.
Recognize the other side
Where a slice of American pie, might be too much to search for.
Therefore, the crust is what we work for.
Through vices and illegal activities while humanizing this behavior as our only identity.
Recognize the other side
Where hate seems to be a part of some people's DNA.
Where apologies are suddenly accepted from racial comments, which encourages half of the world to look away.
Recognize the other side
Before you shoot what is loved by family and friends.
Before you take what is given
and cherish what is material

and die before realizing

how to develop what is spiritual

We have been labeled as the other side....

Another story is being
told and half the world is listening.
Justice is the answer.
Not guilty is
George Zimmerman....

Recognizing the Other Side

THIS IS WAR

I've engaged in a war against my own people.
Convincedly, I thought the problem was them.
Until I looked into the mirror, and here I am.
Inwardly screaming from a self-removal of guilt,
this is one of the many wounds I must heal from.
But this is WAR!
Everyday I'm weary about landing on a mine because every step toward peace, can potentially blow away a piece of my mind.
But this is WAR!
The type of war that's waged when equality between people isn't mutual.
The appreciation for humanity, was at the mercy of a cynic.
If it benefited me,
I deprived them of the
joy, from making an honest living.
This is War!
Retaliation is a given. Either law enforcements or the victims will make

sure, I answer for my actions.

My family will become a casualty of it.... Whether they know it or not.

My reality has become one

of many United States soldiers who went on

tour to Iraq, but never returned.

For the greedy purpose of a war, I couldn't discern.

But this is war!

I don't like it or love it, but

I'm a prisoner of it. Upon my release,

will be a shameful celebration, from family and friends.

Who will be glad I'm home because I fought for something

that I no longer believe in.

That was WAR!

AMERICA

America. My country.
Where it's been predetermined for me
to live amongst the hungry.
Where the strong preys on the weak
in order to survive. Circumstances forced Mothers
to pick up bibles to keep hope alive.
In America.
Our country. Where my ancestors were shipped
across the Atlantic Ocean. Chained by their feet and
wrists, covered in their own feces and urination
and tossed in the ocean
if death rescued them before making it to this
destination....
America,
this monkey,
who rides my back because I'm addicted
to its ways.
Who told me twenty-one is the age when I'll become
a man.

Prescribing us with drugs that disrupt the intellectual
divine we hold within.
America,
not once have I thought to be your friend.
Not once have I felt patriotic.
Your public schools have educated me to be robotic
when employed by your companies.
The history of where I come from,
has been buried by your dishonesty.
This is why I'd rather be respected by my people, than live
for one of your honoree's.
America.

Recognizing the Other Side

WHAT ARE WE

Lost behind the presence of time,
forgotten inside millions of minds....
Who am I to the common people?
Good for now or forever evil?

Found within a dangerous decline, caught without a
presence of
mind.
What am I to a crooked culture?
Balanced or unequal?
Good for now or forever evil?

Death is my destination,
my spirit has proven to be sacred.
Patience is the key to set me free, but I'm captured in a
sincere,
question Who are we?

Life being filled with situations, that only left my soul
for the taking.
Hating the hatred that has locked me into a question of,
What are we?

Delano Walker

AGAINST ALL ODDS

You expect for me

to stay in my place like the spirit that lives

inside my skin.

You prefer for me to stay within, within the

boundaries that society has socially constructed.

Within this space that's so confined that if you were

to measure

my surroundings, it'll be equivalent to a six by nine.

You expect for me to stay in my place, don't raise my

voice and plead

my case.

I take pride in my beautiful black skin.

So, if I told you, I'm unapologetically black,

I said what I meant and I'm not taking it back.

You expect for me to stay in my place, dehumanize

my masculinity,

Europeanize my Afrocentricity and turn my history

into a plain

ol' mystery.

You expect for me to stay in my place, spit in my face

like it's

Recognizing the Other Side

the sixties in America, assassinate me first then
criminalize
my character.
Sadly, your actions will be justified.
Say her name, Breonna Taylor.
Say her name, Sandra Bland.
Say his name, Freddie Gray.
Say his name,
Walter Scott.
Say his name, Treyvon Martin.
Say his name,
Michael Brown,
Say his name, Tamir Rice.
Say his name, Marcus Darcus.
Say his name, Demetrius Baldwin.
Say his name,
Brian Floyd.
You expect for me to not recognize
that you have robbed, stolen and broken people to such an
extent that
the whole world has witnessed it.
You still won't admit
but you expect me to stay in my place?
I can't do that, and I won't do that. I'll be a disservice to

my people.

Furthermore, I can't stand on the shoulders of those who came before me.

Once again, I'll never give up my rights for you all to control me.

If you knew better,

you'd stop provoking me.

MISREPRESENTATION

My mind is in
a constant war with my heart.
My ears worship what my eyes take pleasure in.
We (poor people) can taste success, but what lingers
in the air, smells like
we'll never win.
My neighborhood is suffocating from oppression
while the government is telling
us to breathe by making monthly investments.
He's thrilled by watching the
lacking independence.
He pays the neighborhood schools a visit
to tell the kids they have a chance,
at life!
A life that seems like it exists in his
palms, in all the tricks up his sleeves falls on Black
people who never saw his arms.
A life that we don't know so well because we become
culture shocked
from how others present themselves.
A life that shouldn't allow us to live in between

Delano Walker

because segregation was a reminder,

we're only 3/5 of a human being.

A life that has more questions than answers and

my only question is why we don't deserve an answer?

Because we are negroes?

Because we colored people?

Or is it because we black?

See, regardless of their excuses, we support their

illusions by entertaining

their philosophies.

We descendants of the movement and revolutionizing

ourselves perpetuate

improvement.

But we fight common sense with confusion

and logic is in plain sight.

Yet

…it's useless.

My message to us: Be useful.

it's bigger than us, we represent a people

unless you want to represent a statistic or

be another black man dead for seeking undivided

attention.

Or represent a jail system and be guilty before

Recognizing the Other Side

they think about trying you as a victim.
Whatever you represent, make it obvious that
children are the number one priority
on every continent.
It's been too long and we're still
representing a country that hasn't thought about
representing us....
But wait, I know what we prefer to represent....

CULTURE

I'm from a culture where if you jump off
the porch, your manhood will soon be established.
Uncivilized behavior and devaluing humanity meant
we found ways
to turn up our savage.
This is what we impress upon the community on our
journey towards manhood.
So, the elderly is disrespected.
Ignorance is being protected by
the misconception of what a man is.
Nowadays, the community doesn't ask us what our
plans are.
It's heard in our conversation. We're driven by who is
doing what and trying to keep up with
those lives that seem better on the surface.
As if we were created accidentally and born without a
purpose.
Take a minute and listen to the lives of those who
sometimes feel broken....
On fo' them, I'm high as hell.
On fo' them,

Delano Walker

"He gon' get himself killed
for thinking his people are the only people that'll do a
drill."
Eventually, blood will spill
but the initial target wasn't hit.
Sadly, an innocent child was killed.
This is my culture where our babies are being taken
away too soon and sometimes, they never see the
light of day.
Especially when
they are aborted in the womb.
My culture is Chi Raq. I call it, heroine in the spoon.
A lot of us fiend to be a part of it but it's the worst
drug you can abuse.
I can understand if you didn't tune in.
I'm reporting live with old news, but we'll never win
living this lifestyle.
So, how many more lives do we have to lose?
How many more lives do we have to lose?
Mook, Marcus, Keywon, Keyon…
B4, Shady 4, Kango, Leon, Shawty 4…

JUSTICE

Your tears are justified.

You lost someone you never imagined leaving.

You saw and heard some things

you never imagined experiencing.

Your child is my child.

Yet, I can only imagine what you

feel.

If justice sits on a mountain,

together we should climb that hill.

If justice is not guilty, together we should file our first

appeal.

I need you to know I'm here.

With you and for you, despite these trying times.

The weight from injustice maybe seen physically, but

it'll never alter our hearts and minds.

Delano Walker

I KNOW WHY THE CAGED LION ROARS (PART I)

I know why the caged lion roars.
With nothing to gain, nothing to explore,
battered by a relentless image of bars
that never fails to remind you of where you are.
Where the sun has shed its bright light.
Where tears are shed each night
and the mane has lost its glare
and the spirit is tamed and is fierce-no more.
Rather employed
to safe keep a distant hope.
A hope surely hidden and bravely stored.
Oh, yes…
I know why the caged lion roars.
He roars in hope of the
days when he is caged no more.

I Know Why a Caged Lion Roars
(Part II)

I know why a caged lion roars.
It's taken from a natural habitat
and forced to adapt in a new environment.
Expected to be silent and obedient at all times.
His nature poses a conflict of interest to his trained mind.
I know why a caged lion roars.
This might be his last time, to express pride in what he's being deprived of.
FREEDOM!
Without invasive territorial threats during mating season,
he feels emasculated.
For once, his strength wasn't tested by his own cubs.
I know why a caged lion roars.
His hope never wavers, nor does it budge.
He lives for the day when his life will return back to where it was.
Until then,
the process of healing wont began.
For now, he roars because the divinity inside him won't allow him to hold it in.

ROAR!

Delano Walker

DESTINY CHANGERS

I am picked from a box
by which many others look like me.
We are many colors, nevertheless, we are deadly.
I like to think of
us as changers of destiny.
Filled with the
envy of our possessor.
If the soon to be victim life was great,
we are placed in a chamber to make it no better.
We are changers of destiny!
Once we come into contact with flesh,
we explode.
Piercing arteries
and fracturing bones.
I can promise you this:
Those
filled with hate, can't leave us alone.
We have been used in an assassination of Fred Hampton,
Malcom X, and the murder of Nipsey and 2Pac Shakur.
Imagine now a clean weapon in the hands of the minds
that are so filthy....
Nothing positive is triggered inside these niggers.
Nothing is good inside these folks.
Only a coward approach to take away hope.
We are changers of destiny
who happens to be eyes for the blind.
Who has been used sadly for people to kill their own kind.
Our purpose was to become the stoppers of time.
But as deadly as we are,
we'll never erase these people from millions
of minds:
Nipsey, Fred Hampton, Malcom X,
Martin Luther King Jr., Tamar Rice,
Michael Brown, and 2 Pac.

A State of Mind

Alicia Keys, State of Mind, a diary of
my thoughts expressed eloquently between these invisible
lines.
From this day forward, I hope they'll transcend time.
From this point of view,
I hope to open the eyes of the blind.
Where are we?
Obviously, we haven't went anywhere.
Still, I stare
and see through the miseducated
claim they're not
black, because of a lighter skin tone complexion.
Where are we?
Behind cases
that killed innocent children.
Against the ideas of rebuilding because honor comes
with tearing the neighborhood down.
How could we
be torn between
what's true and what we believe.
Expecting a harvest of success, before we plant seeds
of hard labor. Blind to the real problems,
because we're too

Delano Walker

busy taking it out on our neighbors.
Why are we
fighting to prove
our worthiness to everybody else except our own?
Looking to accompany the privileged, but telling our people:
I rather be alone.
And alone
we remain
because no matter what we do,
to be something we're not
our reality stays the same.
We're all we got.
Alicia Keys, State of Mind, diary of my thoughts,
I expressed eloquently behind these invisible color lines.
From this day forward, I hope they transcend time.
From this point of view,
I hope they open the eyes of the blind.

MONUMENTAL

My hands are raised high.
This is a symbol which one
day should turn into a statue.
To remind the American people,
humanity is common
up until
a darker complexion....
Then we're considered not equal.
This symbol is submission before those who are supposed
to be just yet at the first opportunity,
use excessive force which is the gap that didn't bridge trust
between law enforcement and African Americans.
This symbol is the source we reference to
when our movement is, Black Lives Matter.
This is for those who once was, are here now,
and soon will come after.
We're experiencing a different type of capture,
that's far from the chains our ancestors were confined to.
These bondages are the thoughts of authority,
actions of the enforcer,
and the narrative of reporters.
Our story is not ours to be told.
Our bodies are not ours to cherish.
And our minds are not ours to control.
Yet the rest of us are supposed to feel safe in a skin our
brothers and sisters are no longer alive in.
So, let this statue be a reminder in our most defenseless
posture, in our most helpless gesture and within this
interaction:
We're whole human beings and have been treated like
improper fractions.
And like always, we
have to be reduced to a lower term before being seen as a
common denominator.

Delano Walker

Our hands are raised high so, why shoot?
We are Monumental People Who Deserve a Monument!

BIOGRAPHY

Delano Walker is the oldest of three and a father of three beautiful girls named Ja'Niyah, Myanna, and Harmoni. His childhood and teenage years were split between his mother and aunt who raised him to the best of their ability. As a teenager while living with his aunt, Delano developed a desire of wanting to know what was happening outside. Soon this desire became, not just what he imagined, but a thought he will soon react on. At the age of 17, Delano was arrested and charged with aggravated battery with fireman and armed robbery. Later he was sentenced to 10 years in prison. This is where he developed a deep appreciation for words and realized despite his incarceration, words could liberate him or confine him depending on how he used them. Since he picked up his ink pen, he rarely puts it down.

Delano is what you call a Revolutionary in the 21st Century. He is not afraid to talk about controversial topics. He believes in equality and the betterment of humanity, but also knows you cannot fill anyone else's cup if yours is empty. Along his journey, he discovered the courage to walk in his original form. Through his poetry and his brand Trap Fitness, he seeks to inspire the rest of the world to walk in their original form.

Writing is one of the many gifts God gave him and is what gives him hope. He uses poetry to tell his story. Poetry gives him the freedom to share his perspective on emotive subjects. Partaking in his poetry promotes encouragement and forward-thinking among men and women. Delano plans to continue writing, doing spoken word, diligently working out, and promoting being a black man in America to assist the culture in making it a thing again.

Trap Fitness is a clothing brand he started in the year 2020. Delano wanted the word "trap" to be seen as something positive versus the negative connation the word receives. There were times him and his cellmate spent reminiscing about how diligently they approached various vices they were involved in while being in the hood. They compared it to the way they grinded in the gym. He realized while in the gym they were hustling for physicality, instead of being in the hood hustling for survival.

During Delano's time of self-reflection, he realized all the mistakes he made, all the things he could have done differently. He knew he had to be true to himself and act on his gifts in a way that made a significant impact. Poetry and exercise for him is self-care and a steppingstone to climb the many obstacles of not only black men, but black people, in America today. Delano Walker is the epiphany of a black man in America.

www.ingramcontent.com/pod-product-compliance
Lightning Source LLC
Chambersburg PA
CBHW071913070526
44583CB00016B/1969